Deirdre Underwood.

CONTENTS

Series editor: Tim Carr

BIBLE SOCIETY
Stonehill Green, Westlea, SWINDON SN5 7DG, England

© *Kathy Keay 1990*

First published 1990

British Library Cataloguing in Publication Data
Keay, Kathy
  Women alone.
  1. Bible. Special subjects. Women
  I. Title   II. Hiscox, Rhoda
  220.8'3054

ISBN 0–564–01514–8

Printed in Great Britain

Typeset in Times 11/13 pt.

*Bible Societies exist to provide resources for Bible distribution and use. Bible Society
in England and Wales (BFBS) is a member of the United Bible Societies, an
international partnership working in over 180 countries. Their common aim is to
reach all people with the Bible, or some part of it, in a language they can understand
and at a price they can afford. Parts of the Bible have now been translated into
approximately 1900 languages. Bible Societies aim to help every church at every
point where it uses the Bible. You are invited to share in this work by your prayers
and gifts. The Bible Society in your country will be very happy to provide details of
its activity.*

INTRODUCTION

More than at any other time in history, increasing numbers of people are spending longer periods of their lives on their own: the unmarried, single parents, divorcees, widows – of both sexes and all ages. The changes in legislation which have taken place in our society, even over the last forty years, have radically affected the way we all live. Housing estates are now built specially for "single professionals". Professional women tend to marry later than in previous generations. Many women still feel they have to choose between marriage and a career, and Christian women, unmarried and divorced, often face added dilemmas:

"How can I marry someone who isn't a Christian?"

"There just aren't any eligible men in our churches."

"The Christian men I know like me, but deep down would expect their wife to be more traditional."

To remain on your own rather than marry someone who isn't a Christian is a hard decision to make. So is the choice to live alone rather than live in a shared household, or move into an old peoples' home when you are older. Such choices carry with them long-term consequences which can deeply affect a woman's understanding of who she is and to whom she belongs, as she goes through different stages of her life.

† What does the Bible have to say to women alone?
† Is the "singles phenomenon" a creation of our western world?
† How does a woman alone cope with conflicting pressures from both Church and society – is she fulfilling the feminist ideal or does she remain the Christian misfit?
† What about loneliness and sexuality?

The Bible studies in this booklet are designed to explore these difficult questions.

Being alone often means that you struggle with deep personal issues on your own, too. It's easy to think that everyone else is coping well, when you know that life on your own can be extremely tough.

Whether you enjoy being on your own or not, it is important to approach each of these studies with sensitivity to the other people in your group and a real desire to discover what the Bible says. Before you begin, therefore, commit yourself to honest, sensitive discussion with one another and expect God to speak to you (individually and as a group) through his Word.

AIM

The studies are designed primarily for women who, for whatever reason, are single, though they can be used by women's groups generally, or even by mixed groups (though they may need to adapt some of the questions). Session four will probably be a women-only session.

The aim of each session will be to apply biblical principles and insights to the lives and experiences of the group. Some of the Bible passages included in this series (e.g. the passages from 1 Corinthians) were written in a cultural context very different from our own. Others are more directly applicable to single women today. Group leaders are encouraged to take these cultural differences seriously in a way that prevents group members from coming to simplistic conclusions.

STUDYING THE BIBLE TOGETHER

You may have chosen to join this group because the subject relates to you or interests you, but may not be used to studying the Bible in a group, or you may be used to more traditional Bible study groups. Don't worry! You are not expected to be experts in theology, or to come up with what you think might be the "right" answers.

So much of our contemporary thinking, in Church and in society, presupposes that we ought to be so self-sufficient that we don't need support and encouragement from others. The New Testament, however, offers an alternative model, where learning to love and trust one another is essential, and made possible as people like yourselves meet together to share their lives and experiences.

This book uses relational Bible study methods to examine the issues facing women who for one reason or another are on their own, who want to take a new look at their own lives, and develop their relationships with God and with others more fully.

WHAT IS A RELATIONAL BIBLE STUDY?

Relational Bible studies are for people who want to begin relating more meaningfully to others, and to explore what it means to be part of a wider Christian community.

In many parts of the world there is a new interest in women "doing theology" together. As groups of women meet together, often informally at first, they begin to see how their own experience and insights are important, and how studying the Bible shows them principles to live by, given by a loving God who is intimately concerned about every aspect of our lives.

At the same time there is a growing interest in the idea of women's groups and "community". For some, this is expressed in the development of much closer relationships with a few people, or with friends living in the same neighbourhood. Belonging to some kind of support group or community is particularly important for people who live alone. It is up to each of us to discover where we fit in and what works best for us. Usually this means beginning to share a much greater part in the lives of others, where there is a growing commitment to help support and encourage each other in various ways.

"But I live on my own and have no desire to do otherwise," you may say. Even if this is the case, we all need people to some degree, and joining a relational Bible study group can offer a spiritual alternative to groups very much in vogue at the moment, such as women's psychotherapy groups. In so doing they can become a major source of strength and support, helping you build deeper relationships with others and with God, whatever your personal circumstances may be.

HOW TO USE THIS BOOK

It's best to keep the number of the group to around eight people, since the focus in a relational Bible study is on relating to one another in a meaningful way.

There is a lot of direct teaching in the Bible on relationships. We will investigate this teaching during the course of these studies, and members of the group should be encouraged to speak and learn from their own experience and that of others in the group.

Each member of the group is important. If someone misses one of the studies, then the group will automatically "change shape". If at all possible, members of the group should commit themselves to stick with the course from start to finish, so as to get the most out of the group experience.

Confidentiality is to be respected. It is very important for members to know that anything they choose to tell the group will be kept in strict confidence. Outside the group, anyone is free to tell their own story, but not those of others. Some members, with particular experiences, may need further help or counselling beyond the group. They need to be encouraged to seek this where appropriate.

BUILDING GROUP IDENTITY

When a group of people meet together (even once a week) for six or eight weeks, they form what is known as "a group identity". When Paul wanted to build a group identity among the early Christians he told them that together they were "the Body of Christ". Groups, like people, often have names: the Wednesday Group or the Nineteen Hundred Group. A name for your group may arise naturally. It's important though that groups don't become cliques. New members should be welcomed and made to feel at home as easily as possible.

GETTING STARTED

There is no need for the same person to lead every study. It's good to have variety. You may say,

† "I'm not a gifted leader"
† or a theological expert
† or an organizational genius
† or I'm not a strong Christian with all the answers

Just as well! As each group member has a copy of this book with its step by step instructions, all the leader need do is to say, for example, "Can we begin?" or "What shall we do with the time that is left?" Leadership is not so much a teaching role as an enabling one. This may involve being the first person to talk about your own experience, to encourage other members of the group to join in (if that's necessary). This works very well in many women's groups. It's as we listen to one another that we learn to love, respect, and support one another.

TIMING

Each session will last approximately an hour and a half. The number of questions and exercises will vary in each session, and group members should not feel that they have to look at all the questions. It is more important that aspects of each study are tackled which are most relevant to those present in the group. The activities will include group discussion and creative exercises, e.g. making a collage, writing a poem, or planning a diary.

SYMBOLS

After each study you will see the following symbols:

 something you have learnt about God

 something you have learnt about yourself or human nature

 a new insight

 something to put into practice

 something to do together

Re-read the passage and apply the symbols to what you have read. If you are not going to write in this booklet, keep a notebook to record what you have gained from each study. Bring one with you before the first session. At the start of each new study, write the Bible passage reference at the top of a new page. Date the study so that you can look back and see what you have learnt.

SESSION ONE

IDENTITY: WHO AM I?

Psalm 139

"**M**iserable, wicked me, how interesting I am."
W H Auden

AIM

This study looks at the question of identity. Where do we get our identity from? "What makes me *me*?"

This is particularly an issue for women on their own. So many women see themselves in relation to their husbands or bosses, or the boys and girls they have grown up with. It's easy to think,

"If I am not Mrs X or Mr Y's assistant, then who am I?"

"Basically, I am only what I am expected to be."

TO BEGIN

Spend a few moments thinking about your own life. How far do you feel this is true of you? Turn to the person next to you and discuss.

† List the different roles you are required to play on a daily basis.
† Which do you find easy and which more difficult?
† What would you like to change?

Read the following Bible passage:

This psalm, traditionally believed to be written by David, expresses God's complete knowledge and care for him. Through all of life's experiences God remains faithful,

9

present, and active in David's life. He is the touchstone of David's identity; the source of his life, guidance, and inspiration. This psalm, like many others, can be echoed by Christian believers in every age who have experienced God's reality for themselves.

¹LORD, you have examined me
and you know me.
²You know everything I do;
from far away you understand
all my thoughts.
³You see me, whether I am
working or resting;
you know all my actions.
⁴Even before I speak,
you already know what I will
say.
⁵You are all round me on every
side;
you protect me with your
power.
⁶Your knowledge of me is too
deep;
it is beyond my understanding.

⁷Where could I go to escape from
you?
Where could I get away from
your presence?
⁸If I went up to heaven, you
would be there;
if I lay down in the world of
the dead, you would be
there.
⁹If I flew away beyond the east
or lived in the farthest place in
the west,
¹⁰you would be there to lead me,
you would be there to help me.

¹¹I could ask the darkness to hide
me
or the light round me to turn
into night,
¹²but even darkness is not dark for
you,
and the night is as bright as the
day.
Darkness and light are the same
to you.

¹³You created every part of me;
you put me together in my
mother's womb.
¹⁴I praise you because you are to
be feared;
all you do is strange and
wonderful,
I know it with all my heart.
¹⁵When my bones were being
formed,
carefully put together in my
mother's womb,
when I was growing there in
secret,
you knew that I was there –
¹⁶ you saw me before I was born.
The days allotted to me
had all been recorded in your
book,
before any of them ever began.
¹⁷O God, how difficult I find your
thoughts,
how many of them there are!

¹⁸*If I counted them, they would be more than the grains of sand.*
When I awake, I am still with you.

¹⁹*O God, how I wish you would kill the wicked!*
How I wish violent men would leave me alone!
²⁰*They say wicked things about you;*
they speak evil things against your name.

²¹*O LORD, how I hate those who hate you!*
How I despise those who rebel against you!
²²*I hate them with a total hatred;*
I regard them as my enemies.

²³*Examine me, O God, and know my mind;*
test me, and discover my thoughts.
²⁴*Find out if there is any evil in me and guide me in the everlasting way.*

Psalm 139

Using the following symbols:

 something you have learnt about God

 something you have learnt about yourself or human nature

 a new insight

 something to put into practice

 something to do together

re-read the passage and apply the symbols to what you have read.

TO TALK ABOUT

What does this psalm have to say to women on their own?
Is God's intimate knowledge about you something

† you fear?

† which makes you feel secure?
† which makes you feel uneasy?

How does this compare with your other relationships?

Which particular aspects of this psalm communicate to you most powerfully? Why?

DIGGING DEEPER

Think about your own life.

Write down a particular event or relationship which has left you feeling hurt, undermined, or isolated.

Take time to imagine that Jesus was with you in that situation. He knows all the details of what happened. How can this psalm help you when you next feel anxious or alone?

REFLECTION

† Write down a few thoughts about your own life, perhaps in the form of a poem or the sort of thing you would write in a diary. What is important to you?
† What are your hopes and fears? Is God real in the midst of your experiences of life? If so, how? How would you like God to be more real in your life?

There may be one or two people in the group who are willing to read what they have written to the group as a whole. Others may prefer to keep their piece of writing in a notebook and update it from time to time as their experiences and understanding change.

WORSHIP

Turn what you have written into a prayer or meditation, thanking God for all that you know about him through your own experience. Be honest about areas of your life that still seem unresolved and in which you want to see God working.

SESSION TWO

VOCATION AND WORK: WHAT AM I HERE FOR?

Luke 11.27–28: Romans 12.2–21

"On February 7th, 1837, God spoke to me and called me to his service." *Florence Nightingale*

AIM

The aim of this study will be to explore the nature and meaning of work as it affects our lives. This is particularly relevant to women on their own, as they are usually entirely responsible for earning their own living. Any older women in the group will be able to add their own contribution, too (perhaps of other vocational, or voluntary work).

TO BEGIN

Imagine you are at a party or having coffee at a friend's house. Someone turns to you and says, "Do you have children?" or, "What do you do?"

What is your response? Does either question make you feel undermined?

Share your response with other members of the group.

TO TALK ABOUT

1. If you have a job, how do you see it:

† As a way of paying the bills?
† As a way of using your gifts and training?
† As a vocation?
† As a tedious necessity which you would give up if you could?

Choose one or two of the above. Turn to someone next to you and discuss them.

2. What different kinds of work are represented by people in the group? Are you self-employed, employed by someone else, working from home, working outside the home, in paid employment, or in charity work? What are the pros and cons in each of these situations?

3. What makes a person's work vocational?

4. Do you think women and men have different approaches to work? If so, what can be learnt from each?

The passage below was written by Paul to the church at Rome. Its theme is life in God's service. Its broad, general principles offer wisdom and advice to Christians in every age, whatever their work or background. If we want to know how to live a life that is pleasing to God and life-giving for ourselves, we will find that this passage is just as relevant today as when Paul wrote it.

Read the passage individually or together now.

Don't let the world around you squeeze you into its own mould, but let God re-make you so that your whole attitude of mind is changed. Thus you will prove in practice that the will of God is good, acceptable to him and perfect. (J B Phillips)

2Do not conform yourselves to the standards of this world, but let God transform you inwardly by a complete change of your mind. Then you will be able to know the will of God – what is good and is pleasing to him and is perfect.

3And because of God's gracious gift to me I say to every one of you: Do not think of yourself more highly than you should. Instead, be modest in your thinking, and judge yourself according to the amount of faith that God has given you. 4We have many parts in the one body, and all these parts have different functions. 5In the same way, though we are many, we are one body in union with Christ, and we are all joined to each other as different parts of one body. 6So we are to use our different gifts in accordance with the grace that God has given us. If our gift is to speak God's message, we should do it according to the faith that we have; 7if it is to serve, we should serve; if it is to teach, we should teach; 8if it is to encourage others, we should do so.

Whoever shares with others should do it generously; whoever has authority should work hard; whoever shows kindness to others should do it cheerfully. ⁹Love must be completely sincere. Hate what is evil, hold on to what is good. ¹⁰Love one another warmly as Christian brothers, and be eager to show respect for one another. ¹¹Work hard and do not be lazy. Serve the Lord with a heart full of devotion. ¹²Let your hope keep you joyful, be patient in your troubles, and pray at all times. ¹³Share your belongings with your needy fellow-Christians, and open your homes to strangers.

¹⁴Ask God to bless those who persecute you – yes, ask him to bless, not to curse. ¹⁵Be happy with those who are happy, weep with those who weep. ¹⁶Have the same concern for everyone. Do not be proud, but accept humble duties. Do not think of yourselves as wise.

¹⁷If someone has done you wrong, do not repay him with a wrong. Try to do what everyone considers to be good. ¹⁸Do everything possible on your part to live in peace with everybody. ¹⁹Never take revenge, my friends, but instead let God's anger do it. For the scripture says, "I will take revenge, I will pay back, says the Lord."²⁰Instead, as the scripture says: "If your enemy is hungry, feed him; if he is thirsty, give him a drink; for by doing this you will make him burn with shame."²¹Do not let evil defeat you; instead, conquer evil with good.

Romans 12.2–21
(***Good News Bible***)

DIGGING DEEPER

† What does this passage have to say to women alone in relation to work/vocation?

† Compare verse 2 quoted from the J B Phillips translation to verse 2 in the Good News version.

† Which version strikes you most forcibly? Why?

You may like to look at other translations or versions of the Bible when we look at other passages in the following sessions. Often it is possible to gain new insights by doing this.

† What values do you consider good and what do you consider evil in your workplace? (verse 9).

† Should women alone always open their doors to strangers? What does this verse mean? (verse 13) Think about your own life.

† Have you ever been unjustly blamed for something you didn't do? How did you deal with it? Did you see God working in the situation? If so, how?

Now read Luke 11.27–8

Here Jesus is talking about the way to find true happiness.

²⁷*When Jesus had said this, a woman spoke up from the crowd and said to him, "How happy is the woman who bore you and nursed you!"*

²⁸*But Jesus answered, "Rather, how happy are those who hear the word of God and obey it!"*

It is easy to feel that as a woman your main reason for living is to bear and raise children. After all, your body reminds you all the time that you have this potential.

† What do these verses say to women alone, especially to those who have no children?
† Do we really believe that there are other kinds of lifestyles which can be equally creative for women?
† Can you say this of your own life at the moment?

Using the following symbols:

 something you have learnt about God

 something you have learnt about yourself or human nature

 a new insight

 something to put into practice

 something to do together

re-read the passages and apply the symbols to what you have read.

REFLECTION

Read the following words from the song *Touching Place*.

Christ's is the world in which we move
Christ's are the folk we're summoned to love,
Christ's is the voice which calls us to care
And Christ is the one who meets us there.
To the lost Christ shows his face
To the unloved he gives his embrace
To those who cry in pain or disgrace
Christ makes with his friends
A touching place.

† What would you really like to do with your life?
† Write down what you consider to be your main skills and gifts, e.g. counselling, writing, exercising hospitality.

Turn to the person next to you. Imagine they are a careers advisor. Read out what your gifts are and ask them how they think you could best use them in the service of others. Is this compatible with what you would like to do with your life?
Change roles and repeat the exercise.

WORSHIP

Use *Touching Place* as a prayer.
Pray that God will help you find ways of using your gifts to the full in helping to meet the needs of others.
Write a two-line prayer to this effect. Date it and watch for ways in which it becomes a reality.

SESSION THREE

RELATIONSHIPS: WHO DO I BELONG TO?

John 4.5–30

"A friend is someone who knows all about us and loves us just the same."

AIM

The aim of this session will be to recognize the importance of different kinds of relationships in the lives of women who are on their own. With no immediate partnership (as in marriage), intimacy and suppport has to be found and cultivated in different ways.

An environment of trust will be important before members of the group feel they are able to talk openly from personal experience, particularly in this and the next study. There are often no easy answers. Studying the Bible like this is not meant to push us into unnecessary guilt and a sense of isolation. Rather, we aim to establish a biblical perspective which will offer hope and excitement at the different ways in which God can make his love known to us through others.

TO BEGIN

You have just received a letter to say that a very good friend, whom you haven't seen for a long time, is passing your way and would like to arrange to see you. What is your immediate response? Turn to the person next to you and describe what it is that makes your friend so special. How did you come to meet and how have they been a good friend to you?

Change roles and repeat the exercise.

TO TALK ABOUT

Choose from the following:

PERSONAL RELATIONSHIPS

1. In your experience, what are the most important qualities in a close and lasting relationship?
2. What can be the most hurtful experiences in a close relationship?
3. How do you enable relationships to grow so that they give you a sense of security and mean a lot to you?
4. How does this differ in your close relationships with women and with men?

FAMILY RELATIONSHIPS

1. Who has had the most influence on you in your family? How?
2. How has your relationships with your immediate family changed as you have grown older?
3. How do you deal with conflict in close relationships?
4. What do you fear most in relationships with your family? How can that be overcome?

The following passage comes from John's gospel. It tells the story of Jesus meeting a woman from Samaria. It is striking in a number of ways. Firstly, Jesus as a Jew breaks through racial barriers in order to talk to the woman. Jews usually had nothing to do with Samaritans. Secondly, he breaks through cultural barriers which kept men and women apart in public places. His disciples had gone off to buy food and were surprised to see him talking with this woman when they returned. Yet through this personal encounter, Jesus offers the woman eternal life and a whole new reason for living.

Read this passage now.

5In Samaria he came to a town named Sychar, which was not far from the field that Jacob had given to his son Joseph. 6Jacob's well was there, and Jesus, tired out by the journey, sat down by the well. It was about noon.

⁷A Samaritan woman came to draw some water, and Jesus said to her, "Give me a drink of water." ⁸(His disciples had gone into town to buy food.)

⁹The woman answered, "You are a Jew, and I am a Samaritan – so how can you ask me for a drink?" (Jews will not use the same cups and bowls that Samaritans use.)

¹⁰Jesus answered, "If only you knew what God gives and who it is that is asking you for a drink, you would ask him, and he would give you life-giving water."

¹¹"Sir," the woman said, "you haven't got a bucket, and the well is deep. Where would you get that life-giving water? ¹²It was our ancestor Jacob who gave us this well; he and his sons and his flocks all drank from it. You don't claim to be greater than Jacob, do you?"

¹³Jesus answered, "Whoever drinks this water will be thirsty again, ¹⁴but whoever drinks the water that I will give him will never be thirsty again. The water that I will give him will become in him a spring which will provide him with life-giving water and give him eternal life."

¹⁵"Sir," the woman said, "give me that water! Then I will never be thirsty again, nor will I have to come here to draw water."

¹⁶"Go and call your husband," Jesus told her, "and come back."

¹⁷"I haven't got a husband," she answered.

Jesus replied, "You are right when you say you haven't got a husband. ¹⁸You have been married to five men, and the man you live with now is not really your husband. You have told me the truth."

¹⁹"I see you are a prophet, sir," the woman said. ²⁰"My Samaritan ancestors worshipped God on this mountain, but you Jews say that Jerusalem is the place where we should worship God."

²¹Jesus said to her, "Believe me, woman, the time will come when people will not worship the Father either on this mountain or in Jerusalem. ²²You Samaritans do not really know whom you worship; but we Jews know whom we worship, because it is from the Jews that salvation comes. ²³But the time is coming and is already here, when by the power of God's Spirit people will worship the Father as he really is, offering him the true worship that he wants. ²⁴God is Spirit, and only by the power of his Spirit can people worship him as he really is."

²⁵The woman said to him, "I know that the Messiah will come, and when he comes, he will tell us everything."

²⁶Jesus answered, "I am he, I who am talking with you."

²⁷At that moment Jesus' disciples returned, and they were greatly surprised to find him talking with a woman. But none of them said to her, "What do you want?" or asked him, "Why are you talking with her?"

²⁸Then the woman left her water

jar, went back to the town, and said to the people there, ²⁹"Come and see the man who told me everything I have ever done. Could he be the *Messiah?" ³⁰So they left the town and went to Jesus.*

John 4.5–30

Using the following symbols:

 something you have learnt about God

 something you have learnt about yourself or human nature

 a new insight

 something to put into practice

 something to do together

re-read the passage and apply the symbols to what you have read.

DIGGING DEEPER

Everyone needs relationships with the opposite sex. For women on their own this can sometimes be difficult. People can think they are either *"out to get a man"* or simply *"easy prey"*. Yet Jesus took risks in his encounter with the Samaritan woman, but without undermining or exploiting her.

† How did he do this?

† Do we often *"play safe"* too much in our relationships or, like this woman, have we experienced a number of relationships which have not worked out?

† What did the Samaritan woman learn from her encounter with Jesus?

† What principles does this passage give us for relating across the sexes?

† Jesus knew about the woman's relationships with men, but he did not condemn her. He saw that she was trying to

fulfil her deepest needs through relationships with men, but it wasn't working. (She'd had five men and was now onto the sixth!) How can our relationship with Jesus be developed to become, increasingly, the source of "living water" in our lives?

† You are arranging a party. Write a list of whom you would like to invite, bearing in mind how they might relate to each other. What sort of music would you choose? How formal or informal would you make it? Would it be mixed or women only? Would you have games or leave people to talk amongst themselves?

What do you think are the most important elements necessary to make a really good party "work"? If you don't like parties, what other ways do you celebrate your friendships?

REFLECTION

In the map of relationships below, put your name in the centre and write in other names in each section, near or far, according to how much you feel you "belong" to each other. Where would you place Jesus in this map?

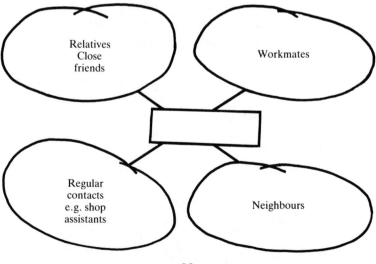

WORSHIP
Pray for each of these people in turn.

Lord, there are lots of holes in my life.
There are some in the lives of my neighbours.
But if you wish we shall hold hands.
We shall hold very tight
And together we shall make a fine roll of fence to adorn Paradise.
                                    Michel Quoist: Prayers of Life

SESSION FOUR

LONELINESS AND SEXUALITY

Song of Songs 3.1–5: 1 Corinthians 7.1–9

"It may well be a case of the spirit being willing, but the flesh being not simply weak, but designed to work in the opposite direction." *Margaret Evening*

AIM

The aim of this session will be to provide a safe environment for individuals to be affirmed in their sexuality by discussing common experiences usually kept to themselves.

It may be important to keep this as a women-only session unless those present are happy to talk openly in a mixed group.

As in Session 3 the aim will be to emerge with a positive attitude towards one's own sexuality in the light of biblical teaching.

TO BEGIN

1. What have you found are the main problems of loneliness (e.g. fear or inability to cope?) Discuss them with other members of the group.
2. When have you felt most lonely? Are there certain factors which contribute to your loneliness, or are they more situation-related, e.g. in large crowds or other people's families, etc?
3. What do you do when you feel lonely?
4. "Singleness OK, but celibacy no." Do you agree with this statement? Discuss your views with the person next to you.
5. How can you express your sexuality at different stages of

your life? How important to that expression is having children?

6. How can you achieve close relationships with people of the same and opposite sex without getting inappropriately involved?

Read the following passage.

¹Asleep on my bed, night after night
I dreamt of the one I love;
I was looking for him, but couldn't find him.
²I went wandering through the city,
through its streets and alleys.
I looked for the one I love.
I looked, but couldn't find him.
³The watchmen patrolling the city saw me.
I asked them, "Have you found my lover?"

⁴As soon as I left them, I found him.
I held him and wouldn't let him go until I took him to my mother's house,
to the room where I was born.

⁵Promise me, women of Jerusalem;
swear by the swift deer and the gazelles
that you will not interrupt our love.

Song of Songs 3.1–5

What are the main points which strike you about these verses?

In the next passage, the apostle Paul is writing to the newly established church at Corinth, a city where immorality and temple prostitution were rife. How were the believers to make the most of their lives for Christ, whilst at the same time living in a place where "sex came easy" if you wanted it? Was it better to marry or not? How can Christians live with their sexuality if they are not married?

These issues are just as relevant today as they were then. The Christians at Corinth had written to Paul about these matters and this is his reply.

¹Now, to deal with the matters you wrote about.
A man does well not to marry. ²But
because there is so much immorality, every man should have his own wife, and every woman should have her

25

own husband. *³A man should fulfil his duty as a husband, and a woman should fulfil her duty as a wife, and each should satisfy the other's needs. ⁴A wife is not the master of her own body, but her husband is; in the same way a husband is not the master of his own body, but his wife is. ⁵Do not deny yourselves to each other, unless you first agree to do so for a while in order to spend your time in prayer; but then resume normal marital relations. In this way you will be kept from giving in to Satan's temptation because of your lack of self-control.*

⁶I tell you this not as an order, but simply as a concession. ⁷Actually I would prefer that all of you were as I am; but each one has a special gift from God, one person this gift, another one that gift.

⁸Now, to the unmarried and to the widows I say that it would be better for you to continue to live alone as I do. ⁹But if you cannot restrain your desires, go ahead and marry – it is better to marry than to burn with passion.

1 Corinthians 7.1–9

Using the following symbols:

 something you have learnt about God

 something you have learnt about yourself or human nature

 a new insight

 something to put into practice

 something to do together

re-read the passage and apply the symbols to what you have read.

DIGGING DEEPER

† How do you think Paul is being realistic or unrealistic about coming to terms with your sexuality?

† What particular problems do women on their own face in the Church today who want to get married but who can't find a suitable partner?

† How might these passages help single people in the Church?
† Do you think single men get "a better deal" from the Church?
† What principles do you think should guide the expression of sexuality for women on their own?

REFLECTION AND WORSHIP

Write on a piece of paper the name of anyone with whom you have had a relationship which has been affirming. Thank God for this person and pray for God's best in his or her life.

Write down the name of a person (if any) who has hurt you or whom you have hurt by being involved sexually with them. Pray for God's healing in your own and their life, and then destroy the piece of paper in front of you. Turn to the person next to you and pray for each other.

SESSION FIVE

RESPONSIBILITY AND CHOICE

1 Corinthians 7.25–38

"Choice – the salt of life which makes much rough fare palatable . . . – a duty which we have no right to evade or to delegate to another."

Problems of the Day 1913, The Englishwoman

AIM

The aim of this session is to emphasize that God has given us the capacity to make choices which we must exercise in every area of our lives. This ability is part of God's gift to us as people made in his image. We do not respond purely by instinct, but by making decisions.

TO BEGIN

You have just got a new job, which means you need to look for a place to live in a new area. A friend who lives there has offered to check the local newspapers and visit any likely places which come onto the market. Turn to the person next to you. What factors will influence the type of place you want to live? Give her a list of points to consider which are both practical and reveal your own personal preference when choosing housing and a home for yourself.

TO TALK ABOUT

1. In what areas of your life have you been most aware of God's guidance? Has this been clear at the time, or in retrospect?

28

2. What would you say are some of the dangers involved in expecting God to guide you in every detail of your life?

3. Give an example of a situation from personal experience where it became clear that God cannot be programmed, i.e. where your prayers were not answered as you expected. What did you learn from the situation about personal responsibility and faith?

4. When you have important decisions to make, from whom do you seek advice? What other factors are involved in helping you to make the final decision?

5. Are there any areas of life where you particularly expect God to help you (e.g. finding the right person to marry)?

6. *"Marriages are made in heaven."* What are your feelings about this statement?

7. Would you ever join a Christian dateline service, asking God to guide you to a suitable person?

In the passage below, Paul continues to give advice to the unmarried and the widowed. He makes it clear that making decisions about marrying or not marrying brings responsibility, so it is crucial to make the important decisions in life wisely.

Now read the passage.

25Now, concerning what you wrote about unmarried people: I do not have a command from the Lord, but I give my opinion as one who by the Lord's mercy is worthy of trust.

26Considering the present distress, I think it is better for a man to stay as he is. 27Have you got a wife? Then don't try to get rid of her. Are you unmarried? Then don't look for a wife. 28But if you do marry, you haven't committed a sin; and if an unmarried woman marries, she
hasn't committed a sin. But I would rather spare you the everyday troubles that married people will have.

29What I mean, my brothers, is this: there is not much time left, and from now on married men should live as though they were not married; 30those who weep, as though they were not sad; those who laugh, as though they were not happy; those who buy, as though they did not own what they bought; 31those who deal in material goods, as though they were not fully occupied with them. For this world, as it is now, will not last much longer.

³²I would like you to be free from worry. An unmarried man concerns himself with the Lord's work, because he is trying to please the Lord. ³³But a married man concerns himself with worldly matters, because he wants to please his wife; ³⁴and so he is pulled in two directions. An unmarried woman or a virgin concerns herself with the Lord's work, because she wants to be dedicated both in body and spirit; but a married woman concerns herself with worldly matters, because she wants to please her husband.

³⁵I am saying this because I want to help you. I am not trying to put restrictions on you. Instead, I want you to do what is right and proper,

and to give yourselves completely to the Lord's service without any reservation.

³⁶In the case of an engaged couple who have decided not to marry: if the man feels that he is not acting properly towards the girl and if his passions are too strong and he feels that they ought to marry, then they should get married, as he wants to. There is no sin in this. ³⁷But if a man, without being forced to do so, has firmly made up his mind not to marry, and if he has his will under complete control and has already decided in his own mind what to do – then he does well not to marry the girl. ³⁸So the man who marries does well, but the one who doesn't marry does even better.

1 Corinthians 7.25–38

Using the following symbols:

 something you have learnt about God

 something you have learnt about yourself or human nature

 a new insight

 something to put into practice

 something to do together

re-read the passage and apply the symbols to what you have read.

DIGGING DEEPER

† What reasons does Paul give here for marrying and for not marrying?

† Are they reasons which you consider important?

If not, what reasons would you give in both situations?

† Have you ever given up a relationship because you didn't feel it was compatible with your Christian faith? What were the issues?

† How do you feel about it in retrospect?

† What (if anything) did you learn and gain from the experience? Discuss this with a partner.

REFLECTION

Write in your diary or in a notebook areas of your life in which, with God's help, you will develop a new or renewed sense of personal responsibility. Write a prayer concerning one matter in particular, which expresses the tension between God's guidance, personal responsibility, and choice in your life. Date it and update it a year from now.

WORSHIP

Read the following prayer written by an Indian woman.

Life not death
I find that your will knows no end in me.
And when old words die out on the tongue
New melodies break forth from the heart.

Rabindranath Tagore, India

Now give thanks for the times when you have known God working all things together for good in your life through the decisions, good and bad, which you have made. Write a two-sentence prayer which expresses these thoughts.

SESSION SIX

AGES AND STAGES: FACING THE FUTURE

Ecclesiastes 3.1–5; Galatians 6.2–10

I am young, and my tomorrows are plenty,
so my faults will not hold me down.
For my faith, though it be weak,
makes me strong.

Robbie Walker: "The Eternal Child"

AIM

The aim of this study is to identify the issues which face women alone at different stages of their lives, and to recognize the dependability of biblical principles when applied to our changing lives and circumstances.

Members of the group will be encouraged to think about their lives (past, present, and future) and to understand the relevance of scripture for all time and at particular ages and stages of life. In this way it is possible to discern one of the ways in which God speaks, recognizing that for everything there is an appropriate time and a season for every activity under heaven.

TO BEGIN

You have just had a phone call to tell you that a parent or close relative has had a stroke and has been rushed to hospital. What is your immediate reaction? Turn to the person next to you and, as with a trusted friend, work out what you would do for the best, in both the short and the long-term.

TO TALK ABOUT

1. What are the issues facing women on their own in their 20s, 30s, 40s, 50s, and over 65? List them.
2. Make a chart illustrating your findings using images from magazines.
3. Which are most relevant to you?

The writer of *Ecclesiastes* recognized that life has different stages, and that within each there are activities which are particularly appropriate. One of the secrets of happiness is to see what stage of life you are in, making the most of its unique opportunities and understanding its pressures. This is especially relevant for women on their own at different stages in their lives.

Read the passage.

¹Everything that happens in this world happens at the time God chooses.
²He sets the time for birth and the time for death, the time for planting and the time for pulling up,
³ the time for killing and the time for healing, the time for tearing down and the time for building.

⁴He sets the time for sorrow and the time for joy, the time for mourning and the time for dancing,
⁵ the time for making love and the time for not making love, the time for kissing and the time for not kissing.
Ecclesiastes 3.1–5

DIGGING DEEPER

Now read the same passage in the New International Version, if it's available. Is there a different emphasis in this translation?

Does God pre-ordain our lives?

What general principles can we see here which are important to understand as we travel through life?

33

The second passage talks about the secret of perseverance and bearing one another's burdens. As we face different stages of life with different responsibilities and pressures, we all need one or two people who will help us along.

This passage is also a reminder that we too have a responsibility towards others.

²*Help to carry one another's burdens, and in this way you will obey the law of Christ. ³If someone thinks he is somebody when really he is nobody, he is only deceiving himself. ⁴Each one should judge his own conduct. If it is good, then he can be proud of what he himself has done, without having to compare it with what someone else has done. ⁵For everyone has to carry his own load.*

⁶*The man who is being taught the Christian message should share all the good things he has with his teacher.*

⁷*Do not deceive yourselves; no one makes a fool of God. A person will reap exactly what he sows. ⁸If he sows in the field of his natural desires, from it he will gather the harvest of death; if he sows in the field of the Spirit, from the Spirit he will gather the harvest of eternal life. ⁹So let us not become tired of doing good; for if we do not give up, the time will come when we will reap the harvest. ¹⁰So then, as often as we have the chance, we should do good to everyone, and especially to those who belong to our family in the faith.*

Galatians 6.2–10

Using the following symbols:

 something you have learnt about God

 something you have learnt about yourself or human nature

 a new insight

 something to put into practice

 something to do together

re-read the passage and apply the symbols to what you have read.

DIGGING DEEPER

† How is this passage particularly relevant to women on their own?

† What is meant by "carrying our own load" (verse 5)?

† How do you achieve the balance between being independent and interdependent with others, especially as you get older?

† How can these principles help you persevere when your natural energy starts running out?

REFLECTION

Read the following meditation.

An old ship's hull
is dreaming
of golden times
when it was
still putting out to sea
when it could roll
in the breakwater
and take the waves
over its bow
without going down.
But I
will not dream
of my strength and youth
of missed chances
and things that were
and were not.

I will calculate
the low and high tides
and put out once more
into a treacherous sea
full of the knowledge
of my unchanging captain.   **Ulrich Schaffer: "Into Your Light"**

† What strikes you most about this poem?

WORSHIP

Now write an honest poem or prayer which expresses your achievements, hopes, and fears as you look at your life, past, present, and future.

† What do you specifically want to say to God in all this?
† What do you think he may be saying to you?
† What difference does it (or might it) make being in relationship with God as you journey through life's various stages?

Make a few notes, then offer your thoughts and comments to the rest of the group.

This marks the end of this series of studies.

Find an appropriate way of thanking one another for the different contributions that have been made during these studies.

You may like to continue meeting as a group and look at other issues covered in this Bible study series in *Women in the Church* by Rhoda Hiscox.